Rosemary Read (handwritten)

- To J (handwritten)
Christmas (handwritten)
Patrick (handwritten)

Imagine

Patrick Purnell SJ

. . . the 'composition' consists in seeing through the gaze of the
imagination . . .

(Ignatius, *Spiritual Exercises*)

Way Books
The Way, Campion Hall, Oxford, OX1 1QS, UK
www.theway.org.uk

First published 2004,
by Way Books, Campion Hall, Oxford,
OX1 1QS

The front cover image is 'Resurrection' by Mark Cazalet

The illustrations at the beginning of each section are photographs of sculptures by Rory Geoghegan SJ

Printed and bound by Antony Rowe Ltd, Eastbourne

British Library Cataloguing-in-Publication Data
A catalogue record for this book is available
from the British Library
ISBN 0 904717 14 3

Contents

FOREWORD

 There are moments of serendipity when a chance encounter leads to a moment of surprise. This has been my joyful experience of Patrick Purnell's poetry. I was introduced to his imaginative and reflective style by a mutual friend, and with his permission I quoted from his poem 'The Christ Child Tumbled' in my televised Christmas address from Wells Cathedral in 2002:

> The Christ-Child tumbled
> Into the world head-first,
> Caught by a nimble midwife
> Felicitously,
> Who thumped him promptly
> To gulp the air and cry.
> This was the first known sound of God
> In the world.

His insight about the midwife's thump revealing 'the first known sound of God in the world' spoke deeply to me, and to many who watched the programme.

 Patrick's style invites people into those ordinary moments of life, and reveals their meaning and significance simply and profoundly. In 'Christmas Is Being Put Away', his evocative description of decorations being put back in the box and of 'Mary stashed in tissue paper, Joseph wrapped in a woolly hat . . . All tucked away under the stairs', says it all in terms of this annual happening in a million homes. But what makes the poem resonate is the observation:

> We'll climb another year
> Up to bed and down to breakfast.
> And somewhere in the pantry of my thoughts,
> A wistful coil of questions
> Goes unanswered.

And haven't we all been there? Our Christmas reverie opens for us unanswerable, sometimes unbearable questions, to which somehow only the ritual of decorations and crib offers answer.

+ Peter B. Price
Bishop of Bath and Wells

INTRODUCTION

'Imagination is evidence of the Divine'

William Blake (1757-1827)

It was in a bygone age that I was first introduced to the Spiritual Exercises of Saint Ignatius, and that introduction was not particularly fortuitous. It was a time when those who handled the Exercises would, with the best of intentions, pump as much spiritual information as they could think of into their retreatants' heads. We had five talks a day, nearly every day for thirty days. It was not until thirty *years* later that I really began to understand the Spiritual Exercises, when I made them under the guidance of a director, one to one. This for me was a turning point, a revolution and a revelation of the Spirit at work in my life. I learnt to discern the movements of that Spirit. Many of the poems in this collection are closely linked to the dynamic of the Exercises and, especially, to the contemplations of the life of Jesus.

One of the tools of the Spiritual Exercises is the imagination. 'Imagine', says Jesus at one point, 'a sower going out to sow. . . .'. Imagine! Imagination is a true way of knowing; it can be thought of as *'the access to the real through the unreal'*.

Sometimes, I know, my imagination runs away with me, and I begin to wonder whether the imagination is a tool which I use, or whether I have become the tool of my imagination. The poems write themselves. It is a strange experience. A line appears from nowhere, leading to another and yet another; the lines tumble out, I know not how. I do not know how the line 'Allowed a womb-wick light to glow' in the poem on the Incarnation emerged—I only mistily understand it, yet it speaks to me of what I can only describe as the undertow of the Spirit's guiding presence.

✳ The imagination can lift the past into the present; it can also project us into the future. We come to terms with what we have been; we grapple with what, under God's grace, we can become. We contemplate the Gospel Word as he lives, acts and teaches; we contemplate how this Word might change us and direct our steps towards a fuller life. Imagination is at the heart of conversion. We change, not because of doctrinal argument or moral persuasion, though both have their place, but because the imagination calls us into a new future and offers us an incentive to change. Imagination offers us images and pictures of how the pieces of our lives could fit together in a completely new way. This, I believe, is precisely what happened in Jesus' own life. Brought up in the traditions of his people, he was steeped in their stories. What obviously fascinated him was the Kingdom story, which had begun with Samuel and had continued right down to his day. In the hands of the prophets, the concept of the Kingdom changed: no longer was it a narrowly nationalistic territorial venture, but rather a dream of all peoples on the planet living together in peace, truth, justice and love, and sharing the resources of the earth. This dream Jesus made his own. He put together the pieces of his world in a completely new way. 'The Kingdom of God has come near', he said. The Kingdom he proclaimed was the fruit of his imagination.

✳ As servants of God's kingdom, we struggle to bring God's transforming love to the world. We have a need, therefore, to know something about what we are doing. The imagination supplies this need. It is our imagination we bring to bear on the world around us, and in so doing we shape and transform not only what lies outside us, but also our own selves. The active use of the imagination reveals a God at work, creating and liberating the world.

✳ Imagination enables us to picture reality in a new way. Imagination enables us to remake reality, to discern something different from what appears at first glance. Imagination is more than a day-dreamer's flight from reality. Imagination is more than the irresponsible fantasy that fabricates an image in order to evade reality. Imagination is having the courage to think and say something new. The tantalizing question: 'What would happen if . . . ?' has given birth to inventions, to revolutions, to new social movements. And only imagination can answer it.

✳ Imagination fuels the virtue of hope. Hope is the dynamic of the unfulfilled self. Hope is more than mere optimism. Hope is not the expectation that something will turn out well, but rather the certainty that something makes sense, regardless of how it turns out. Hope is rooted in God's power to make use of humanity's folly. Hope is to believe that the future is benign.

✳ I was born in Wales, and whenever I manage to cross Offa's Dyke I feel at home. For my childhood holidays, we used to motor up from Cardiff to a big house called Mia Hall, outside Dyserth. This house had a chapel-of-ease in its grounds, and occasionally, a priest from Saint Beuno's used to come and say Mass on a Sunday. Saint Beuno's also figured in my mother's life. As a girl she was a boarder at the Convent in Rhyl, and was a close friend of the daughter of the Leach family; Mr Leach, at that time, was the bailiff of the Saint Beuno's farm. It was on that farm she spent many of her holidays, round about 1905. It was at Saint Beuno's that in 1941 I entered the Jesuit novitiate, and there I stayed until the summer of 1945. Today it is a Spirituality Centre where I frequently go, either to give the Exercises or to make my own retreat. Saint Beuno's is perched on the side of Maen-Effa, with magnificent views of the Clwyd Valley. Saint Beuno's has straddled my life. I have loved it and hated it at varying times in equal measure. It has had a great influence over me. This explains why one of the few longer poems in this collection is entitled, simply, 'The Valley Of The Clwyd', and why much of what I present here was written there.

✳ The poems which appear in this collection are the fruit of the imagination. They have been written over a period of some forty years, but only about half a dozen have ever been published before. Now in my greying years there is time; and so, encouraged by my friends, and with the support and opportunity given me by my brethren, I am offering my friends and brethren these poems. I also feel I have a duty to acknowledge my ability to write. That this is gift, I have no doubt. But it has taken me perhaps some sixty years to recognise it.

Patrick Purnell SJ
De Nobili, Southall, 2003

My special thanks go to Michael Barnes and Philip Endean for their encouragement and for their support in the production of this book.

I

Some Verses About
God,
About Whom
I Know
Very Little

The Greeting

Haven't You The Wit . . . ?

Why do you keep pestering me,
Scratching at the window pane?
Leave me be!
Why do you ferret me out,
Scenting me in my burrow maze?
Stop bothering me!
Why do you scour the place for me,
Like a householder looking for a thief?
Haven't you anything better to do?
I'll hide myself from your preying eyes;
You'll never find me,
I'll disguise myself!
You'll never recognise me.
I'll deceive you!
You'll be at a loss
To know what to do.
Give me peace!
Haven't you the wit
To see I cannot cope with you—
With you who have earmarked me
For life?

The Price

. . . the scribe said to him, 'You are right, Teacher; you have truly said that "he is one, and besides him there is no other"; and "to love him with all the heart, and with all the understanding, and with all the strength", and "to love one's neighbour as oneself",—this is much more important than all whole burnt offerings and sacrifices'. When Jesus saw that he answered wisely, he said to him, 'You are not far from the kingdom of God'. After that no one dared to ask him any question.

Mark 12.32-34

'Why have you come,
Proclaiming you're Messiah,
Disturbing our neat and ordered lives
Of sacrifice and psalmody,
The morning and the evening prayer,
The yearly journey to Jerusalem,
The billowing clouds of incense smoke,
The fatted calf, the paschal lamb,
The oil poured out, the basket full of corn?
What more do you want our Deity to have?
Our purses bare and empty?'
And he unrolled the parchment scroll
And cried aloud the words he read:
'I have come to set you free,
To lift the burden of the Law,
To open wide the prison gate,
To loose tongues that are dumb,
To sight the blinded eye,
To make the lame a-dancing go,
And make the lepers clean.
What more do you want your Deity to do?'
'We'd like to ask you, Sir', they said,
'What coin we pay
For this good news?'

The Hermit

For seven and twenty years
She had walked the causeway every morning,
As the sun broke the rim of the sea,
Or the rain tapped her sandalled steps.
A half-mile out, a half-mile back to the hut that was her home,
Back to the long haul of morning prayer.
The air that day was summer bent in her hair,
The gulls looped and swooped over the crested waves;
Oyster-catchers and cormorants waded in the shallow beach water.
Where was God that day
As the sea swirled and leapt around her aloneness?
She never questioned her need to be there,
In this place on the edge of her world.
Driven? No!
She hadn't been driven.
There had been no compelling,
No 'should', no 'ought'.
Only a laboured 'Yes',
As if she had been giving birth to herself.

But to whom? To what had she said 'Yes'?
The prayer stool floated on an unknown sea,
As she sat within the silence of her soul
And felt the cry within her, dry in the salt air.
What stayed with her, as her mind danced,
In the shadows of the flickering candlelight,
Was the utter strangeness of God.

It was, as if each time she came to prayer,
She had to cross a frontier,
Assume an explorer's role,
And travel a country she had never walked before.

God was so strange!
It was not a strangeness evoking fear
But of curiosity, edging her on
To discover a new vocabulary,
New definitions of the familiar:
Mercy, peace, justice, love.
These had always lodged in her heart's mind,
But here, in the hollow scooped out by her yearning,
Seemed to make no sense,
But only added to her bafflement.
'Love!' How the word eluded her!
Love was the sea's underbelly,
The constant flow of the waters, heaving and groaning
In the immensity of their tidal power,
Crashing on the causeway rocks,
Catching her, holding her,
Plunging her into the darkness of its depths,
Where she felt utterly secure.

Sometimes her eye was drawn to the icon beyond the candlelight.
What held her were the eyes.
She registered in her mind the hands—
How the writer had placed them;
The book they held; and the folds of the robe.
But it was the eyes set deep in the bearded face
Which at rare times thrust her into a stillness
She struggled to comprehend.
It wasn't simply a stillness of not doing,
Of being in repose;

All her faculties were sharply attuned,
Like a bird on a branch readying itself for flight.
What she experienced then (how could she put it?)
Was an attraction, a being drawn out of herself
By a someone she couldn't name.
What did it feel like being looked at by those eyes which held her?
She had no words to describe it.
It wasn't an appraisal;
There was nothing quizzical about it,
But (and it was this which astonished her)
Those eyes were filled with wonder.

When she reflected,
There seemed to be a kind of space
Between where she was
And where she placed God,
A space she breached by her desires and yearning,
By her sighs and, at times, by her tears,
But there too, fanned out, was the clutter
Of the props she used —
Mantras, rosary beads, candles,
Devotions, holy water, holy writings, icons —
To bridge the divide
And attain the unattainable.

She knew deep down that what she wanted
Did not reside in what she did,
But it lay in the emptiness of waiting.
'I sat in the Tower,
Waiting,
Waiting for the sun to rise;
That it would, I knew,
But the sand in the hour glass
Remained poised,
Delaying the passing of time.'

The Sea Flows Across

The sea flows across
The shore of my innermost being,
Then ebbs and flows and ebbs yet again;
Flowing and ebbing, up and down,
Gracing the wide empty beach with its water;
Now smoothly, now beaten by the wind,
Churning up the grit and the gravel,
Mixed in the sun-browned grains of sand.
Sometimes (it happens rarely) it seems
As if the ebbing and the flowing halt, cease!
And a vast stillness takes hold
Of the sea and the air,
Almost as if someone was holding their breath,
Motionless!
No bird rustles the breeze
And not a sound — silence!
And in that moment, that fleeting inch of time,
In a peace which has no translation,
Your sigh betrays your presence,
As the flowing and the ebbing of the uncertain sea
Sweeps,
Once more, across the shore.

II

Some Verses About Jesus,

Who Revealed A God

We Couldn't Have Expected,

Still Less

Hoped For

Amazing Birth

Incarnation

And the Word became flesh and lived among us . . .

John 1.14

(i)

There is a darkness unlike other darknesses,
So heavy, so impossibly dense
That it is impermeable to light,
(Or so it seemed)
But it was in this darkness,
The darkness of Creation's corridors,
That a speck, a mote of light,
Smaller than the paring of an infant's nail,
(New moon-shaped)
Astonishingly appeared.

(ii)

It was on a Tuesday, not a Monday,
Of that I am sure;
Mondays I see my sister;
Coffee, morning chat.
And it was mid-morning.
The sun was hot;
This was the time-point
Within the 'before' and 'after'
— The where were you when . . . —
You know what I mean,
When Empire signifying human power
(The First is First, the Last is Last)
Dissolved, and darkness trembled,
As God, crouching over a nascent Universe
Allowed a womb-wick light to glow
And infiltrate the fabled darkness.

Mary

. . . how Our Lady, nearly nine months pregnant (as we may devoutly think of her) and seated on a donkey, with Joseph and a servant girl, taking with them an ox, set out from Nazareth for Bethlehem to pay the tribute which Caesar had imposed on all those lands . . . to see with the eyes of the imagination the road from Nazareth to Bethlehem, considering the length and breadth of it, whether it is a flat road or goes through valleys or over hills . . .

Spiritual Exercises 111-112

Becoming is a winter occupation.
The road stooped down the hill into the long winter valley,
Leaving behind the faces, the houses,
And the well in the middle of the village,
All that was familiar and known to her;
She ventured into the unknown, an adventure,
Along a road she had not stepped before
Into a land bereft of bud,
It being the cold season of the year.
At night as she lay on the flat earth,
The stars, brilliant in the brittle air,
Danced in her sleepless eyes,
As the words of promise played in her ears,
And she felt the child move in her womb.
Such a hard journey! Such a long journey
From a past mottled by the music of David's harp
To a present she trembled in the making;
But she knew it was in the 'now',
In the slow, stumbling, weighted steps she took,
That a new psalm was being conceived,
A melody devised, and words
(Or was it just one word?)
Conjured up from the deep recesses
Of the Spirit's indwelling, groaning to be set free.
Becoming is a winter occupation.

The Dreamer

Her husband Joseph, being a righteous man and unwilling to expose her to public disgrace, planned to dismiss her quietly. But just when he had resolved to do this, an angel of the Lord appeared to him in a dream . . . .

Matthew 1.19-20

'I could see him in the sunlight,
Shadowed by uncertainty,
With disbelief upon his face,
Lifting his head as if to shake
Out of his mind the pain of doubt and dark despair,
And soothe the sadness of his soul.
I had no power to ease his heart,
No skill with words
To lift the veil of mystery,
And tell what had been done;
Naught could I do but suffer his suffering,
He in whom my future trembled;
But it was weariness
Which stilled his sorrow,
And in his sleep the dream began.'

Shepherds

In that region there were shepherds living in the fields, keeping watch over their flock by night. Then an angel of the Lord stood before them, and the glory of the Lord shone around them, and they were terrified. But the angel said to them, 'Do not be afraid; for see—I am bringing you good news of great joy for all the people: to you is born this day in the city of David a Saviour, who is the Messiah, the Lord. This will be a sign for you: you will find a child wrapped in bands of cloth and lying in a manger.'

Luke 2.8-12

O maniacal night, I bless you!
I bless you, moon, for your ponderous dance,
And you, the stars, for breaking your light
Into a thousand myriad pieces.
I bless you, wind, for your thunderous power,
And, you, the Angels, streaking the skies
With your mad and magical voices.
We took to our heels with the wind in our hair
And the luminous prophecy burning our ears.
We drove the rooks from off their perches,
And sent their nightmares squalling
Over trees leafless in their winter bereavement.
The owl shrieked in frenzied terror,
As we jumped the fence
And sent the hare a-squealing.
We chased the cow across the field,
And called the fox and the squirrel to join us.
And gentle night was leaving her bed,
And the light from the East was lapping the town,
When we paused at the threshold,
And breathed in the air,
And sighted the scene the Angels had told us.

The manger was there!
We smiled at the maid,
Cracked a joke with the man,
And grinned at the child
Who had burrowed his way
Through ancestral mazes,
And tumbled in through the womb of a maid,
To ferry the living across the channels of death,
And quieten the owl in its frenzied pleading,
And give to the rooks the sweetest of dreaming.

The Question

In those days a decree went out from Emperor Augustus that all the world should be registered. This was the first registration and was taken while Quirinius was governor of Syria. All went to their own towns to be registered. Joseph also went from the town of Nazareth in Galilee to Judea, to the city of David called Bethlehem, because he was descended from the house and family of David. He went to be registered with Mary, to whom he was engaged and who was expecting a child. While they were there, the time came for her to deliver her child. And she gave birth to her firstborn son and wrapped him in bands of cloth, and laid him in a manger, because there was no place for them in the inn.

Luke 2.1-7

If you come with a 'when' question,
I'll answer;
If you ask 'how' or 'where',
I'll tell you;
But if you come with a 'why' question,
I'll not know.
If you ask, 'When was he born?'
I'll answer,
'4 BC, give or take a year or two'.
If you ask, 'How was he born?'
I'll tell you,
'Like any other human being'.
If you ask, 'Where?'
I'll answer,
'In Bethlehem in the land of Judah'.
But if you ask, 'Why?'
I'll be silent,
As I stand amid the rubble
Of a manger and a cave
And of a world
His Father loves so much.

Christmas Is Being Put Away

Christmas is being put away:
The Kings in a cardboard box,
Mary stashed in tissue paper,
Joseph wrapped in a woolly hat,
And the Infant Christ in a nylon sock;
All tucked away under the stairs,
We'll climb another year
Up to bed and down to breakfast.
And somewhere in the pantry of my thoughts,
A wistful coil of questions
Goes unanswered.

John The Baptist

Sign-posted, he stood
Thigh deep in the river water,
At the gathering of the roads.
Some came holding long spears, helmeted,
Others, poor, untaught, ignorant of God's ways
Stood silently by.
Women, too, were there, hiding in dark veils,
While others, learned and bearded, stood sceptically,
Asking questions of the expectant air:
'Which way?', 'Where?', 'Why?', and 'Who knows?'
Were there answers in the tumbling stones
Which they had not heard in their reading of the Book?

While he, who had encountered truth
In his mother's womb,
Plunged each body into the flood,
As it poured over the stickle stones,
Crying, 'Repent!', 'Repent!', over and over again,
And pointed a finger away from himself,
To another, whose sandals he felt unworthy to touch,
In whom he could read
Humanity's future in spirit and truth.

III

Some Verses
About
The Ministry
Of Jesus

Pietà

He Was With Wild Animals

In those days Jesus came from Nazareth of Galilee and was baptized by John in the Jordan. And just as he was coming up out of the water, he saw the heavens torn apart and the Spirit descending like a dove on him. And a voice came from heaven, 'You are my Son, the Beloved; with you I am well pleased'. And the Spirit immediately drove him out into the wilderness. He was in the wilderness forty days, tempted by Satan; and he was with the wild beasts; and the angels waited on him.

Mark 1.12-13

He curled his body
On to a ledge
In the cave's black centre,
High above the prowling beasts
His ancestor once
Named in Eden's Garden,
Sniffing the scent of his fear.
And it was there,
Where he had made himself secure,
An alien voice,
Gentle and soft as balm,
Using his customary speech,
Coiled itself round the cave's ribbed roof,
And glided down its dank walls,
Pressing itself upon
His inner mind, and whispered,
'Not you!
You are not *God's* Son!
How could you be?
You are *my* Beloved!'
And terror locked on fear,
(The white of his eyes
Displaced the darkness)

And the scent of his dread
Baited the beasts.
And he . . .
There was nothing he could do,
But clutch the memory
Of the great white winged bird
Plunging out of the sun on to the earth's surface,
As water
Trickled down
His face.

The Crossing

They came to the other side of the sea, to the country of the Gerasenes. And when he had stepped out of the boat, immediately a man out of the tombs with an unclean spirit met him. He lived among the tombs; and no one could restrain him any more, even with a chain; for he had often been restrained with shackles and chains, but the chains he wrenched apart, and the shackles he broke in pieces; and no one had the strength to subdue him. Night and day among the tombs and on the mountains he was always howling and bruising himself with stones.

Mark 5.1-5

The moon was dark,
Dark was the journey,
Dark the waves,
Fear the colour of the wind.
Leaving behind what was tried,
Crossing the border
Foraging in uncertainty.
He made the journey,
Ramrod,
Looking neither right nor left,
Into the howling torments
Of the pieces of a man
Chiselling his body,
Like a deranged sculptor
Defacing his work of art.
And he, the Creator's Son,
Who knew the draught of what it was
To be a man,
Trembled.

The Well And The Woman

She never saw him again,
When she walked to the well
To draw water.
Each day, every day,
She searched
For the sight of him:
Would he be there?
'My heart is a pool of waiting—
Perhaps, just perhaps,
Tomorrow he'll come,
And ask, "Give me to drink!"
You've laid hold of me
Like the scent
Of the jasmine flower.'

The Water Stones

When evening came, he was there alone, but by this time the boat, battered by the waves, was far from the land, for the wind was against them. And early in the morning he came walking toward them on the sea. But when the disciples saw him walking on the sea, they were terrified, saying, 'It is a ghost!' And they cried out in fear.

Matthew 14. 23-26

There was tumult in the waters,
Wind valleys of sea tumbled the boat;
Fear was the in-breath of each sailor man.
Waves shrieked through the rigging;
High, high they reared,
Patterned with faces
We'd known in the village,
Long lost at sea.
Ghosts menaced our sight;
They tormented our ears,
Wailing their souls in their sodden shrouds.
Mist clung to the spray, veiling our eyes,
Vaulting a tomb for the cries of our fears.
And into the cave he came walking,
Walking on the water stones.
Fear buckled to terror.
'A Ghost! It's a Ghost!'
Petrified we clung to the rails,
And he came walking,
Walking on the stepping stones.
Reason lost its moorings, a mad man's cry:
'Bid me walk on the waters, too!'
We tried to restrain him as he stepped overboard.

Crashing the breakers, heavy the swell,
As he stepped on the mountains,
Till the mountains gave way
And panic gouged a scream,
From his heart, lodged in his mouth.
'Save me or I drown!
I drown!
I drown!'
And he, with fleet of foot,
Fretted the ears of the curling sea horses.
And plucked him up by the scruff of his neck,
Out of a waterlogged locker,
And you could hear his laugh
Over the cymbal sea resound,
'How little a faith, you've got!' said he.
'How little a faith, you've got!
You've got
You've got!'
And he laughed at the monstrous sea.

Sweet Clown

Sweet Clown,
You blessed the cup,
Gave thanks to God,
And passed the cup
Among those
Who sat at table;
Each took the cup,
And raised it up
To catch your eye
And nervously they spoke
The customary greeting:
'Long life to you!'
They drank your health
In the blood you'd shed,
Whilst they shredded the bread
You had made your own,
And ate the life
You gave away.

Pietà

They lifted him down
From the arms of the cross,
And caught his body as it crumpled to earth.
'Make way', said the rich man,
'I've crossed a few palms;
He'll lodge in my tomb, newly hewn.'
But she who had only a womb to offer
Ferreted her way from the back of the crowd,
Through the worthy citizens drifting away,
To cuddle the criminal fruit of her womb
As she cuddled him once in a Bethlehem night.

What lives in your womb, O Mother of failure,
As you crouch in the dust under the Gallows Tree?
Mingle the blood and the water, too,
Make clay with the crimson crumbs of the earth.
And you who've housed creation's maker,
Give birth to a new creation,
Where the powerless and the abandoned poor
Find a kingdom home, which you fashion with love.

Failure is the crucible of love;
It is in the very shit
Of human wretchedness
That the seeds of love and love's fidelity,
Are sown, take root, and come to burst the frightened earth
Of 'I' and 'you' and 'we',
Because only when there's no reason,
No cause, no debt, no call upon duty
Is love what love is.

Mary Magdalene

I walked. I ran,
Sorrow tapped the fleeting swiftness of my feet,
Breaching the Holy City walls
To where our ancestors slept entombed,
Tears held the light from my eyes.
I fumbled-felt my stumbling steps
To where they had laid him, my Beloved:
Better a dead body to wash with tears
Than that void his absence left;
Better his wounds to pierce my heart,
Than wistful memories that melt in the air.
But where? Where? Where? Where are you?
Where? Oh! Where are you?
The vacant slab, the empty tomb!
My heart stands still in the aching day,
While a gentle breeze plays in the trees.
'Why do you weep? Oh! Why do you weep?
The winter is past, flowers appear;
The fig-tree has put forth its fruits.'
Listen! Listen! The Beloved calls;
(His voice in the scents of the vine blossom)
'Mary! Mary!'
He opens my heart
And the sun breaks the day into a myriad pieces,
While the angels ascend and descend
Upon him whom I adore,
Whom I clutch with my arms,
As the voice of the turtle dove announces the Spring.

What Would The Future Be?

After the Sabbath, as the first day of the week was dawning, Mary Magdalene and the other Mary went to see the tomb.

Matthew 28.1

They just stood,
Still,
With their spice-filled baskets,
Staring, horrified,
Eyes out into the deep emptiness
Of the garden tomb,
(Tombs hold their dead)
Wits frozen,
Feet rooted to the ground;
The sheer incongruence of it all,
The terror of impossibility!
Memories of promise,
Heard but not believed,
Hung in the morning sun.
What if it were true?
What would the future be?

IV

Some Verses
About
The Journey
We Make
Searching
For God

The Gift

The Valley Of The Clwyd

Enter the valley at Dyserth.
Take your time and leave a space
Between you, yourself, and where you come from;
Put your foot, for it is by foot you go,
Upon the road that leads to Cwm,
And bless yourself upon your journeying,
For you must consecrate your senses
For what you are about to do.

The ordered houses, each with its own name,
Give way to unattended banks of weeds and hawthorn hedges.
Yarrow, lush ferns, dandelion and buttercup,
Close in upon you like a silent corridor.
At Cwm you hear Welsh voices
Place words like notes upon the air,
And memories of a once accepted grace
Begin to stir within your heart,
And so you take yourself to task.
You carry with you all that makes you what you are,
The love that you receive and give,
The sudden bursts of unexpected joy,
The fears and anguished thoughts,
The hurts within your heart,
That make you stumble on your way,
And leave you with a great unrest;
You stand and feel the valley at the hedgerow break.

How lovely is your valley, Lord God of hosts!
The trees, the fields, the cattle, the birds upon the wing!
Blessed are your people there!

Rhuallt is a station church upon your way,
The crossroads of the busy world,
The world you can't escape from, come what may,
Breaks in upon your silence,
Speaks of need, its need — the world's need;
And in the thorn bush by the fence
The voice of that other World, the Third,
Like a plaintive thrush murmurs inconsolably,
'Eli, Eli Lama Sabachtani?'
And in your helplessness you look upon the valley.

How lovely is your valley, Lord God of hosts!
The trees, the fields, the cattle, the birds upon the wing!
Blessed are your people there!

Perchance there is no answer,
No 'Yes', no 'No', no dream, no cure, no God,
And the grey stones on Maen-Effa's mountain
Witness to an eternal lie,
And the valley goes down to the gates of Hell.
Kyrie Eleison, Christe Eleison, Kyrie Eleison.

I met a cripple on the road
With whom I passed the time of day.
We spoke about the roots and rootlessness
Of all the valley folk,
Of faith and trust and callous insincerity,
Of birth and death, of love and hate,
Till I left him with a storm approaching,
And sheltered at the churchyard gate;

And there I read the beaten stones,
As the blackened clouds descended
To enfold that tiny hamlet
In a wet wind from the West.
Here a Jones and there an Evans,
Each one rotting in the ground
He'd strode or tilled or built upon,
But now had naught to do but wait
For harvest and the yielding of the dead.

How lovely is your valley, Lord God of hosts!
The trees, the fields, the cattle, the birds upon the wing!
Blessed are your people there!

The leaden sky did lift an inch,
And the sun did touch the hills,
But all the same I knew full well
That the limbs of the poor are as thin as reeds
And their bellies are round as berries.

How lovely is your valley, Lord God of hosts!
The trees, the fields, the cattle, the birds upon the wing!
Blessed are your people there!

Bodfari takes you to the valley bed,
Where you yield yourself unto its rhyme,
By narrow roads which twist and turn,
Now left, now right, then left and right again,
By villages with names beyond your skill to say;
And patience, the little that is yours,
Slows you to the Elwy's flow.
You lose yourself and have to guess
Where you are and who you are,
From the rhythm of the mountain tops;

And then it matters not at all
That you do not know yourself
And cannot finger where you are;
All you have—and you don't want more—
Is the valley's peace, which eases you along.

How lovely is your valley, Lord God of hosts!
The trees, the fields, the cattle, the birds upon the wing!
Blessed are your people there!

You leave the silence of the lanes,
And put your feet upon the streets
Where Ruthin people buy and sell
(And cheat the Taxman if they can),
And all the time they love and hate,
Like men and women everywhere.
They meet in shops and round the corner,
And talk about the price of eggs,
The love affairs of those they know,
The raffle for the spastic kids,
The goings-on in foreign parts,
And who is born and who is dead;
And they grey and age together,
Held within the valley's peace.

How lovely is your valley, Lord God of hosts!
The trees, the fields, the cattle, the birds upon the wing!
Blessed are your people there!

And who are you in this valley of grace,
And who do you say you are?

Saint Beuno's

This is a place of God-thoughts,
Where mind composes images,
While heart unknots the sense
Of what was, what is and what could be.
Ifs and Buts grow more subtle,
As the grey stones of Beuno's grow greyer still.
The impossible seems more impossible.
'Leave us on the straw grass
To recite the declensions,
We never properly learnt
Of how we might attain self-mastery.'
And yet within its Annotated Avenues,
Grace, that wild spirit, beckons
To joust once more, (such is grace),
With matters beyond our reach,
The Possibility,
That nothing is impossible.

Feelings

'Follow!' Follow the voice that is calling:
Pick up the echoes from the valley side;
Stir memories of graces once given;
Touch the place where you last knew the way,
But were filled with the darkness of doubt;
Listen to the stirrings within you;
See the movement of shadow and light;
Recoil from the fears that beset you;
Treasure the truth deep within.
Will you stay in the boat protected securely
By rules and commandments traditionally preached,
Safe when the scales are balanced at judging,
Sure of a place with the just?
Or will you trust yourself to the pull of your feelings
And walk on the waves of the sea,
Not knowing if it's Christ who calls?
Will you risk all for fullness and freedom,
With only the white stick of love for your guide,
When you're blown by the wind, the sea and the tide,
Because you are sure you've heard a 'Come'
From the voice of the one who once bid you his 'Peace'?
And you take to the waters and dance
In the storm by the light of his face.

Why Have You Come So Early?

Why have you come so early
To this dark December corner,
Crouching prayer-wise in those polished pews?
Why have you left the comfort of your beds
And made your way across the morning streets
To wreathe the city with your sighing?
Words across the altar
Nod against the thoughts of pensioned men
Praying their ageing years away;
Of grandmas musing over siblings;
Of a wife at odds with her man;
Of a stray youth propped by chance
Between his childhood and his manhood state.
Why have you come so early?
Is it that now heaven's market-place is open
For you, and you, and you to make an easy buy?
'Do this for me: and I'll be here for you'.
Will a thousand masses be enough to bring us peace
And will you look with kindness upon our frailty?
Why are you here in this market-place
Of Gospel, wine and bread,
To hear a word you've heard before,
To take the wafer Christ upon your lips,
And catch some droplets of his Blood?
What will that do for you,
As you merge with the people of the street?

Cathedral

She crouches, wizened and gnarled,
Like an old lady of wrinkled beauty,
On a trimmed English lawn.
Her great buttressed arms
Carry stone upon weathered stone
And lift her slender spire to the skies
With a casual daintiness of youth.
Sunlight from windowed tracery
Colour-patterns the graveyard floor,
Where clerics and worthy burghers,
Entombed, snooze in peaceful bliss.
Altars of bread and wine
Hide in dark corners.
Hushed voices probe inscriptions,
Searching for meaning, seeking sense.
Click, click, a polished heel, a whiff of scent, an intruder
Makes her way through a foreign land.
Neat chairs set out for Evensong
Nod towards the choir stalls,
Await the faithful few
With plastic bags from Tesco's down the road,
While men and women clamped to her sacred sides
Stare out at you from their hallowed faces,
Wondering what you are doing
Seeking the living God among the dusty bones of time.

Prayer

(For Liz)

Prayer is by nature elusive.
You can put all the pieces together,
Ready yourself,
As you would to welcome a guest
'Delighted you could come!'
And the guest fades away on the door-step.
You're mistaken!
There was no guest. It was but a mirage.
You run through the process once more,
Making sure you've left nothing out,
And you are left with the tea and the cakes.

Where are you? I long for you to come.
Why are you so difficult to find?
Is there some secret I'm not privy to?
Do you give the key to but a privileged few?
I sit and wait like the lone dawn bird
For the first rays of your sun,
Knowing you are not to be sought for or found,
For you are the seeking,
You are the finding.

Prophets

Prophets are ridiculous, uncomfortable,
In any decent company.
They breathe an air compounded of
Nostalgic dreams and visions,
Mixed with the stench of barn-yard infidelity
And the human lust for power.
Prophets live margin lives,
Impelled by fears they can't control;
Questioned by their inability
To work the epic sign;
Pursued by earnest seekers after truth;
Harassed by those who've learnt the truth;
And driven by the One
From whom they flee
For whom they long.
There lies the paradox:
A collusion
With the perpetrators of human criminality,
(Every prophet is a criminal at heart);
A compassion
For their victims' strangulated lives,
(Every prophet is a victim by design).
There's the tension:
Between the actuality
And the unarticulated truth
They hold within their souls;
Between what's written
In the heart of God
(Which they are darkly privy to),
And its literal translation.

V

Verses

About

This And That

The Song of Songs

An English Church

The place is full of the dead.
Tattered flags high in the raftered ceiling
Droop lifelessly over slain men;
Stony Knights encased in armour,
With scripted scrolls to tell their deeds.
Crusaders spread on granite slabs
Clutch shields embossed with arms
They once carried in some savage war.
All are dusty dead,
Dead as the Crucified upon the wall.
This one they got out of a ditch,
Pierced by a random arrow;
That one they found in a leafy lane
Gouged by a blunted sword;
That one they put together on a dusty road
Shattered by a cannonade;
All they found of him was his head,
Lolling on the window ledge of a French farm.
There's scarcely an acre
From which men haven't picked up a corpse
And lodged it in some English church.
The dead lie everywhere, across sanctuary and aisles,
And burrow deep into the great stone walls.
Windows of remembrance,
Tell of great wars and lesser conflicts,
Aggressive wars and wars of protestation,
Religious wars and wars of dynasties,
Each remembered in the Warrior's Home.

Rolls of honour faded and beribboned
Smugly name dead heroes,
Who killed and were in turn killed
For King, Country, Honour, for God,
And for dreams of peace and islands of tranquillity.
The bugle, pipe and drum of war
Linger in the summer air,
Where men toiled in sweat
To fashion with symmetry and grace
A shrine, to house their God,
Who in violence created peace.

Saint Ignatius

He stumbled into God by accident.
Soldier he was, battle-wound festering,
Bored with its mending, idly reading,
He daydreamt himself into laurels of fame.
(How the ladies would swoon at the sight of him!)
But that dream drained his soul,
Unease gripped his heart ,
While strange men in haloes pushed into his mind,
Trafficking in truth they gleaned from God's word,
Suffering and dying for what they proclaimed,
Beginning to appeal to his embattled soul.
Laying aside his breast-plate and helmet,
He grasped the staff of a pilgrim man
And donned the shift of the poor,
To battle alone with the daemons shadowing his soul.
There in his cave he gaped at visions
Of a love no lady had ever stirred in his soul,
Of a world that confounded his own,
Where cripples leapt and jumped for joy,
Dumb men cracked jokes to deafened ears,
And fishes paid the public tax:
A kingdom far beyond his dreams — the very dream of God.
They came to him from far and near,
Fired by a passion he couldn't check,
To be his company, to set the world ablaze,
Proclaiming Christ to everyone,
Be they Christian, heretic or infidel.
While he ensconced himself behind a garret desk,
Exchanging quill for his battered staff
And read the letters they did send
And wrote with care an answer to each one,
Guiding each with wisdom he'd acquired

By listening to the Spirit deep within,
Who had once touched his lips to frame a prayer
To his gracious Lord and Master holy:
'Take, Lord, and receive all that I am!'
And that same Master, not to be outdone,
Made him his Knight
And as the years buckled under him,
Ignatius wrote his epitaph:
'To the greater glory of the one and only God!'

Saint Francis Xavier

'Modest fame and sufficient gold:
Not too much to ask for a doyen of Navarre.
I was content,
Life was fair,
Till you with your gammy leg,
And friendship in your eye,
Kept pestering me with your kingdom talk.
You gave me visions; shared your dreams;
And I sailed the turbulent seas to Goa.
There with a bell I called the poor
And told them that the news is good,
That they are the well-loved citizens of God.
But that same God had given me prophetic feet.
I could not rest upon one shore,
And journeyed through Malacca and Mulucca,
Staying awhile with those who fish for pearls.
I crossed the wind-swept sea to Kagoshima
And in a world I did not understand
And in a language I had yet to learn
I cried "Christ!"
And still the Spirit did not give me rest
Till I reached another shore.
And now upon Sancian Isle
The Spirit bids me rest.
And all I can do is let the dream
That drew me out from fair Navarre
Enfold me in its embrace,
As I lean upon the mighty walls of China,
Beyond which I have pitched my heart.'

Francis was born in the castle of Xavier, near Sanguesa in Navarre, on 7 April 1506. He died on the island of Sancian, near the coast of China, on 3 December 1552.

Roberto De Nobili SJ

1577 – 1656

What was it that drew you
To disengage yourself
From the story that had nurtured you,
To don the ascetic shift,
To hitch the cord of ceremony across your shoulder,
And with your thumb
Anoint your head with sandalwood?
What made you leave the smiling hills of Montepulciano
And sit cross-legged in Madurai town,
With their sacred texts upon your knees
And search for grains of truth with prayer and penance?
You did not invade the country of their beliefs
With long-lashed words of condemnation,
But gently allowed each shard of truth,
Hidden within the strangeness of a foreign script,
Entry into your soul's self,
There to yield itself to the gospel light.

What urged you to this alien land?
None but the one in whom
There is no alienation.

Having been sent to the Indian mission, de Nobili adopted the dress of a Hindu ascetic and followed the traditions of the Brahmins, retaining their codhumbi (tuft of hair) and cord (cotton string slung over the left shoulder) and adorning his forehead with sandalwood paste.

A Mass Grave

'The remains of hundreds of bodies have been uncovered at a site near Hilla in one of the largest mass graves. Relatives of victims have converged to scour for bodies of political prisoners killed after a Shia Muslim uprising against Saddam Hussein in 1991.'

Newspaper Report

Like a child I ran,
Tossing aside the red dust at my feet,
Up to the brink of the pit,
And there, aghast, I stood
Unable to grasp what I saw,
As the earth disgorged its dead.
They were there shrivelled in huddles,
Hundreds upon hundreds, past counting,
Each ragged in their cotton shifts ,
Each with a bullet in their head,
While the girls in the West, glittered in fashion,
Tripped the cat-walk of silver and gold.

An arm raised, pointed to heaven,
A head gouged of its eyes,
While, before me, blood, dried by the sun-wind,
Congealed on faces like oil,
Hardened by the merciless sun,
While the men of the West travelled the roads
In Jaguars made for speed.
And over it all and within it all
The putrid fumes of flesh baked in the sun,
Hung within each breath I took.

A wailing there was, a piercing grief;
A woman crying loss and emptiness
Drenched the air with her sobs,
For the arms of the man who had folded her once,
While the girls in the West assailed their fans
With trivial songs of love.

There a father keening the air with sorrow
Clutching the pouch he'd given his son
To celebrate his coming-of-age,
While the men in the West gave shares in oil
To their sons in their nineteenth year.

And out of the carnage walked a child
With the face of a woman, ravaged by grief.

Refugees

Stealthily, we moved from the edges,
Drawn by dreams of plenitude,
Leaving our homes at the margins
Of the deserted flatlands,
Where nothing grows,
And what we had of wheels and cogs
Rusts and harbours cobwebs.
It was fear that urged us on,
Hacking at our hearts,
Fear of a demented power,
That fed upon its own illusions,
And cut the navel string
Which bound us to our Tribal Story.
We were stripped at gunpoint
At the precise point of intersection
Between what passed as the frontier of nations.
We carry nothing with us,
But the golden memories
Of a love that had once bound us together as a people,
The incense of a gifted race
Which had tilled a fruitful land for a thousand years,
And we carry, like a sacrament,
The myrrh of our Nation's woundedness,
In which is mixed the wisdom of our ancestors.
This is who we are.
These are our gifts as we stand before your walls,
And if this be not enough to gain entry to your land,
Let the sun come down upon our dry bones,
And the moon carve us a grave.